The Vision Tree
Selected Po

SELECTED POEMS
The Vision Tree

Phyllis Webb

Edited with an Introduction by Sharon Thesen

Published with the assistance of the Canada Council.

Talonbooks
P.O. Box 2076, Vancouver, British Columbia, Canada V6B 3S3
www.talonbooks.com

Printed and bound in Canada by Hignell Book Printing.

Fourth Printing: August 2006

National Library of Canada Cataloguing in Publication Data

Webb, Phyllis, 1927–
  Selected poems

  Bibliography: p. 160
  ISBN 0-88922-202-9

  I. Thesen, Sharon, 1946– II. Title.
III. Title: The vision tree.
PS8545.E2A6 1982   C811'.54   C83-091030-1
PR9199.3.W42A6 1982

ISBN-10: 0-88922-202-9
ISBN-13: 978-0-88922-202-1

Table of Contents

Introduction

Voice

The designation "West Coast writer" often brings to mind, if not the radical shift in language and line away from the modernism of the Eastern Canadian writers of the 1950's and 60's and toward the projective and the redefined sublime of a new, post-modernist verse, at least an identifiable source and stance. By source, I mean the consciousness of language as physical, a materiality prior to the devices of content; and by stance, an abandonment of the dubious privileges of the poet's ego. The concerns and quarrels attendant upon these poetics have been working themselves out in the most interesting writing of the last two decades, including that of Phyllis Webb. What distinguishes Webb's poetry is the quality and range of its operations within a lyric mode, and the formality of its energies. As for voice, that important modifier and signature of style—and taken here in its literal sense— Webb's is notable for its resonance and flexibility. It is an effective voice, informed by the training gained by her extensive work as a broadcaster for the CBC. Not expressive in a histrionic and hortatory sense, Webb's voice is nonetheless a dramatic one. As listeners, we feel spoken to; as readers, we are brought to the poem's senses by the strong measures of her lines:

> . . . When I think of his hymning
> Puritans in the Bermudas, the bright oranges
> lighting up that night! When I recall
> his rustling tinsel hopes
> beneath the cold decree of steel,
> Oh, I have wept for some new convulsion
> to tear together this world and his.

Line

Elements of the precision and beauty Webb demands of her line (and of her line-breaks) are sorted out in her essay "On the Line," where William Carlos Williams' concern with the literal reappears transposed as *the* formal concern of the poetics in her adaptation of one of his most astonishing short lyrics: "So much depends upon: the wit of the syntax, the rhythm and speed of the fall, the drop, the assumption of a specific light, curved."[1] The poem is here called upon to speak unholy knowledge that necessitates redemption, but in formal terms, the concern is movement and shape, what the poetic line *makes* by virtue of its being a poetic line (and not the ornamental railway to virtuous thoughts). Webb speaks of "the seriousness of the moving line, for me"[2] and again what comes to mind is W.C. Williams' instruction that "The goal of writing is to keep a beleaguered line of understanding which has movement from breaking down and becoming a hole into which we sink decoratively to rest."[3] We can all think of poems which pitch headlong and satisfied into these holes—usually the result of a naive formalism or a naive anti-formalism. The attentiveness to the process of shaping, the curve and stretch of the voice of her line across the grid of the lyric, is what constitutes Webb's formality. It has, profoundly, to do with craft, the *working* of the poem at which Webb is so adept.

Ends

Phyllis Webb's poems are able to elicit gratitude in the reader. And what we are often most grateful for are the poem's open completions, which do not stop the poem, but which cast their strange felicity back over all the other lines, so that the whole poem is gathered into a unity without proposing a closure. We are not let down by Webb's endings, but, as if caught in a complicated jazz progression, neither are we permitted the satisfaction of conclusiveness, of argument upheld. The felicitous ending gratifies us because it respects our instinct for a truth which is inseparable from its present particulars. While this kind of completion provokes only satisfaction in the suspicious, who "knew it all along" and who, in reading, wish only to be delivered from the particulars of experience, the *gratitude* provoked by such a recognition of truth (i.e., the surprise of experience), is always an opening:

A long line of baby caterpillars
follow their leader from the house corner
heading dead on for the Japanese Plum Tree.

Take away my wisdom and my categories!

Desire

Webb's lines are as much a gathering in as a winding out. Perhaps only a comedian has a better sense of timing, for "the wit of the syntax" as Webb has it, is to be found in the subtle, intelligent silences within the phrasing and during the line-breaks:

This makes me want to sing. Caw caw.
Or cry.

It is from the line-breaks that all the inventiveness of the poem springs, that is, that point at which all energies re-gather, inspire. In this way, the poem is re-formed at every instance of a new line, composing the energy of transitions, rather than an enthusiasm for an expressible idea. "The Place Is Where You Find It" is both exegesis of the poem's process and documentary of its teleology: in behavioural terms, suicide; in poetic terms, the place the poem (poem seen here as act) comes to at the end of its lines, its energies, its desire:

What was the path she took?
As winding as her gut
with the pain in it?
Along the beach?
To the caves in the hill?
Path of her mind turning
on symbols. Civility and
the Wild Woman's scream.
And horror. Horror.
Path to the beach
at full moon at last
joy of that mean water
the manic ride out in the bay.

Both desire and despair arise from the discrepancy between what we believe the world to be and what it apparently is. By ridding ourselves of desire, we also rid ourselves of despair, or so say the wise. Or, if the world does not cooperate with our desire, we can counter the despair of what it refuses us, by naming it. In the fifth poem of "A Question of

Questions," Webb begins by admitting:

> The error lies in
> the state of desire
> in wanting the answers
> wanting the red-crested
> woodpecker to pose
> among red berries

and ends by asserting the appearance and taxonomy of the "posing" woodpecker. In the course of the poem, thinking, knowing, "head-travelling," and headlessness are the routes of desire that lead to the incarnation of its object, in the form of an image which is capable of being named. Only when something is made visible do we know what it was when it was invisible. Desire must be anterior to thought; thought to the process of disclosure; and what is disclosed is often as much a surprise to the poet as it is to the reader:

> . . . wanting the bird
> to be still and
> wanting it moving
> whiteflash of underwings
> dazzling all questions
> out of me, amazement
> and outbreathing
> become a form
> of my knowing.

Decorum

Not faint-heartedness, nor a penchant for polite beauties only, the decorum of Webb's verse is suspended in its diction, not in its subject matter. The *Naked Poems* are distinguished most of all by their restraint, even their reticence; hence their interest from the reader's point of view. A completely naked body, said Roland Barthes, has no erogenous zones. Thus, the concern of these poems is not desire, but rather the creation of a palpable "otherness." In an early poem, Webb has already referred to the "ambiguous nakedness" of poetry:

> Poetry, the poet's curse
> will look, for better or for worse
> like a simple monk in meditation
>
> cloaked in apparent deprivation:

in its ambiguous nakedness
glows the raiment of its otherness.

Decorum is an attitude of respect for the consciousness of other things, including that of language and poetic diction. By the same unconcealed humility her sense of beauty, and the beauty of her poems, is fuelled: "If I have known beauty / let's say I came to it / asking."

Composure

Webb closes *The Sea is Also a Garden* (1962), her third book (which recalls H.D.'s *Sea Garden*, and which opens with a quotation from Williams), with the desire (which she shares with Ezra Pound), "to elude / The Great Iambic Pentameter / who is the Hound of Heaven in our stress" and to write, if not Haiku, "long lines, clean and syllabic as knotted bamboo." To these ends, Webb set to work on two books: *Naked Poems*, and a book of long lines determined by larger narrative and historical concerns. The envisioned book of long lines hasn't yet materialized, but *Naked Poems*, in which haiku-related forms and sensibilities are consistently practised, was published in 1965. In subsequent poems, Webb returns to the lyricism of her earlier work, now having shed the formally patterned stresses that characterized much of it. The interest in haiku itself, and other Eastern forms, can be attributed to the disposition of Webb's mind, that it seems always to be *moving toward composure*.[4] So that while the exquisite management of tension effected by haiku is present in her writing, we are spared the imitation of its syntax. While Webb's concerns are passionate, her poems are never linguistic or ideological battlegrounds: whatever they might be saying, we are aware of an energy composed inside the diction and consciousness of the poem.

I

Even where the "I" is the subject, the "I" is in flux—not a point of reference but a moving line. "I" appears in its essential transience, moving toward sweet haven or dread exposure:

The light is mauve
my eye's iris blooms
into the nightmare of
riderless horse, the sleep honey
sings through the lilac
and I smell ash.

In Webb's poetry, the first person singular is simply a device that rhymes with "eye". Identity is not an issue in this poetry, to the extent that the "I" is hardly noticeable upon an initial reading of any poem in which it occurs. Even in *Naked Poems*, where the subject is subjectivity itself, the self views the self caught in the "eye" of the other. Both distortions and accuracies occur wherever the speaking "I" travels. "I said / I lied" are equally true, as in:

> Then you must go.
> I sat cross-legged
> on the bed.
> There is no room
> for self-pity
> I said
>
> I lied

The eight-poem sequence "I Daniel", Webb's most recent work, is a careful rendering of the "I" as persona. The permutations are numerous: Daniel as *animus*; *animus* as persona; "I Daniel" repeated as insistence on the persona; "I" and "Daniel" as twinned personae of the same person (Daniel and/or Webb); and "I Daniel" as the way the biblical Daniel refers to himself when reporting on his visions. Webb's reference to the bicameral mind identifies this division as internal. The double appellation "I Daniel" indicates both separation and identity, corresponding to the right and left hemispheres of the brain: the one that imagines and the one that speaks. Who is servant and who is master are questions that the poem (and Daniel) puzzle over, not the least of which is the relationship of the artist to "jobs and treachery and money." This concern with identity as persona has become one of the most engaging in Webb's work, as some of the texts informing this poem indicate: the biblical *Book of Daniel*, E.L. Doctorow's *Book of Daniel*, Timothy Findley's *Famous Last Words*, Julian Jaynes' *The Origin of Consciousness in the Breakdown of the Bicameral Mind*, and Webb's own "Sunday Water: Thirteen Anti Ghazals" from which "I Daniel" takes and further modifies its ghazal form.

Disclosure

The sensuality of Webb's imagery, coupled with the reticence and composure of the poems, are what invite us into their intimacy. The tone of intimacy, of sensuality, is achieved by the play of engagement and disengagement in the lines. There is pleasure in the disclosure of the secretiveness of things, their hiddenness and inviolability. But such dis-closures lead always, and immediately, to the Otherness of the thing disclosed:

>Speak to that violet
>>or call to the light

>and what is given back
>>is not echo
>but the mute substance
>>of the work of love.

Singularity

If the poems are "the mute substance / of the work of love," so are the silences. Webb has not been a prolific writer, but neither has she written carelessly or presumptuously. Hers is the classic pattern of the growth of a writer: the transparency of formative influences (one might single out Yeats and the Metaphysical poets) in the earlier work is steadily subsumed and transmuted (via the bridge of the Eastern inspirations) into a texture that is singularly Webb's voice, rhythm, and attitude:

>. . . And if you catch me resting
>beside the stream sighing against
>the headlines of this pastoral, take
>up your gun, the flowers blossoming
>from its barrel, and join this grief, this
>grief: that there are lambs, elegant black-
>footed lambs in this island's eschatology,
>Beloved.

Shadow

"All time is sadness but the heart is not / unmoved in the minute of the dancing measure." Much has been made of the expressions of personal anguish in Webb's poetry, of her terrible silences, of her preoccupation with (and proximity to) suicide, of her poetics of failure. However, her canonization as a sort of priestess of pain hasn't, I think, been warranted. Webb's candour — both in her poetry and in her prose — about the difficulties of her vulnerability, has invited some curious looks into her psyche, some decidedly more competent and respectful than others, but all seeking to explain the sense of loss, futility, and despair that her poems document. The error of such psychologizing, of course, is that it seeks to identify the origins of this sense of loss in terms of a personal grief, whereas more often than not it is anguish's human universality that is expressed. The presence of despair in a writer's work can often be attributed to the homely fact that, to paraphrase Kierkegaard, the writer is distinguished from the non-writer by the former's ability to make his despair important. As Webb notes:

> The poet in his vision tree
> imparts immaculate necessity
> to murder, ignorance and lust.

It is true that "murder, ignorance and lust" often shadow the poems, but they shadow the poems in the same way they shadow our lives: the darkness simply figures, as presence, in most responsible minds.
For Webb, darkness tracks even the physical act of writing:

> is there a shadow following the
> hand that writes
> always? or for the left-handed
> only?

> I cannot write with my right.
> I grasp what I can. The rest
> is a great shadow.

Because Webb seems to refuse disparagement as a method of expressing her disgust and bewilderment, she is confined to the positive expression of images of pain, such as we see in "Treblinka Gas Chamber," in the "Poems of Failure," in "Prison Report." The structure of the question is often Webb's solution to the problem any writer has of how to speak about pain without exploiting it. But the question can also be used as a form of torture, as Webb discusses in her CBC script "The Question as an Instrument of Torture," published in *Talking* (Quadrant Editions, 1982). The self-torture of the unanswerable "Why?" begins the sequence of poems "A Question of Questions" in *Wilson's Bowl*. The portrait, "Socrates" ("even his last words / a question"), the speculative mapping of the suicide in "The Place Is Where You Find It", and the dismay of:

> Three?
> Mile?
> Island?

in the section entitled "Crimes", are all testimonies to the mystery and the ubiquitousness of human cruelty, pride, and despair. But this no more defines Webb's subject matter than, for example, the redemptive dreams and visions, the witty and perceptive portraits, the preoccupation with mutability in the early lyrics, the terribly private pain of *Naked Poems*, or the loveliness of nature. Indeed, the compelling quality of Webb's poetry is an authority, which stems from an authenticity of experience, not the psychological categories of its passions.

The Vision Tree

In the shamanic religions of the peoples of north-eastern Europe, northern and central Asia, and the Americas, the world is imagined as structured around a great central tree. The poet's relation to this world tree is like that of the shaman's to the magical tree, Tree of Life, or sky-ladder by which he travels between all the worlds composed in this imagination. The vocation of the shaman—transcendence, propitiation, magical flight, healing, and enchantment—is earned by suffering, isolation, dream, ecstatic trance, and song; his initiation and subsequent performances often taking place in the top of a tree, or on a bird-topped pole or ladder. Webb's poem "In Situ" pictures the poet as a shamanic figure in his initiatory crisis or professional derangement:

> With laughter on his haunted face
> a madman captive in a leaf's embrace
> the poet wildly shakes his tree . . .

and as well, in his wise equilibrium:

> The poet in his tree of hell
> will see life steadily and see it well.

The tree's rootedness in the ground, its yearly regeneration, its receptiveness to birds (unborn souls), its beneficence, verticality, and height make it universally apprehended as both *axis mundi* and link between the gods, humankind, and the dead. In the confines of the boughs of a tree, or with his tree-image ritual devices, the shaman, like the tree itself, mediates the celestial, terrestrial, and chthonic realms. Webb's conception of the "poet in his tree" suggests the shamanic vocation of the poet as messenger of the other, as spiritual adept, and as "seer" of visions. From his transcendent viewpoint and despite various states of mind, the shaman/poet in Webb's poem repeatedly observes that "The world is round. It moves in circles." This refrain occurs four times, introducing another aspect of the world tree: its transposition to mandala form. C.G. Jung points out that "an image which frequently appears among the archetypal configurations of the unconscious is that of the tree or wonder-working plant" and further, that depictions of trees "often fall into symmetrical patterns that take the form of a mandala."[5] Jung sees the mandala as the tree (self) imaged in cross-section. Its symmetrical pattern is related to the cross in the Judeo-Christian tradition, a quaternity in form if not in substance, for the tree embodies the process by which the four elements are united. In Jung's discussion of "the philosophical tree" in *Alchemical Studies*, he recalls the tree's special connection with water, salt, and sea water:

> The philosophical tree usually grows alone and "on the sea" in the Western Land, which presumably means on an island. The secret moon-plant of the adepts is "like a tree planted in the sea."[6]

"Wilson's Bowl", the ancient petroglyph bowl carved into the shoreline rock of Salt Spring Island, can be seen in this context as the "moonplant," the mandala configuration of Webb's vision tree. The bowl too represents a quaternity; as a rhyming and linking device, it too joins the celestial and chthonic realms on a surface of earth and water by floating the sun and moon in its stone basin. Like the various treeforms of the shamanic ritual paraphernalia, the bowl is also a technology of the sacred. Webb insists upon its mystical and transcendent potency:

> This is not a bowl you drink from
> not a loving cup.
> This is meditation's place
> cold rapture's.
> Moon floats here
> belly, mouth, open-one-eye
> any orifice
> comes to nothing
> dark as any mask
> or light, more light / is
> holy *cirque*.

The bowl is micro-cosmos, a soul, in which male and female principles are wedded:

> Serene, it says silence
> in small fish

cups a sun
holds its shape
upon the sea

The lance and the cup of Christian mythology find their pre-Christian counterparts in the marriage of tree and bowl in Webb's poetic iconography. Both are sources of life; both are fixed and eternal centres; both are holy. The sequence of poems under the group title "Artifacts" are spirit-poems involving the mythology of native peoples in a more conscious way than in the early instance of "In Situ", an act of the imagination. But Webb as poet is performing in these poems, as well as in others, the shamanic role as interpreter, to the living, of the knowledge of the dead. This is how "the great dreams pass on / to the common good."

Finally

Webb's art is humane, felicitous, and almost unbearably competent. The seriousness of her work belongs to the long tradition of the sublime, and as such it is a function of her sense of vocation. The bewildered, the geniuses, the dreamers, the suicidal and the helpless are given voices in Webb's poetry, with the great consideration and detachment that avoids appropriation of their terror and energies to ideological certainties. Webb resurrects the Unicorn in a lovely poem that declares the reality of its presence, alongside everything else in the human imagination, and affirms once more the fragility and the necessity of the heart in the poet's vocation:

> I know this is scarcely credible now
> as we cabin ourselves in cold
> and the motions of panic
> and our cells destroy each other
> performing music and extinction
> and the great dreams pass on
> to the common good.

Sharon Thesen,
Vancouver, B.C.
July, 1982.

19

Notes

[1]Phyllis Webb, "On the Line", *Talking* (Quadrant Editions, 1982), p. 66.

[2]*Ibid.,* p. 70.

[3]W.C. Williams, quoted in rev. of Paul Mariani, *A New World Naked* in *New York Times Book Review*, Nov. 22, 1981, p. 34.

[4]I take this phrase from Joseph Riddel's book on Wallace Stevens (*The Clairvoyant Eye*, Louisiana State University Press, 1967).

[5]C.G. Jung, "The Philosophical Tree," *The Collected Works of C.G. Jung* (Princeton University Press, 1967), Vol. 13, p. 253. See also Joan M. Vastokas, "Shamanic Tree of Life", *artscanada*, Dec. 1973/ Jan. 1974, pp. 125-50.

[6]Jung, p. 308.

from TRIO

The Colour of the Light

I.

On the apparent corner of two streets
a strange man shook
a blue cape above my head,
I saw it as the shaking sky
and was forthwith ravished.

II.

A man bent to light a cigarette.
This was in the park
and I was passing through.
With what succinct ease he joins
himself to flame!
I passed by silently noting
how clear were the colours of pigeons
and how mysterious the animation of children
playing in trees.

III.

When a strange man arrays
a dispassionate quality before
his public, the public may be deceived,
but a man's strange passion
thrusts deeper and deeper
into its fire of dispassionate
hard red gems.

IV.

And the self is a grave
music will not mold
nor grief destroy;
yet this does not make refusal:
somehow . . . somehow . . .
shapes fall in a torrent of design

and over the violent space
assume a convention;
Or in the white, white, quivering
instability of love
we shake a world to order:
our prismed eyes divide such light
as this world dreams on
and rarely sees.

    I thought I saw the pigeons in the trees. . .

Chung Yung

The year has come round full circle,
All evidence, both external and internal,
Is now proven and visible;

Love has known all seasons,
Cycles within cycles have given birth
To words, patterns, moods
And placed their worth
In necessary violence
Or in absolution.

Purchases have been made
Wisely or imprudently
Neither all being lost
Nor all gained;

Balance, delicate
Yet fibred,
Proves a pivot
Around which are described
Immaculate arcs.

The Second Hand

Here, Love, whether we love or not
involves the clock and its ignorant hands
tying our hearts in a lover's knot;

now, whether we flower or not
requires a reluctance in the hour;
yet we cannot move, in the present caught

in the embrace of to be or not;
dear, shall we move our hands together,
or must we bear the onslaught

of the tick, the tock, the icy draught
of a clock's arms swinging themselves together —
or now shall we kiss where once we laughed?

all time is sadness but the heart is not
unmoved in the minute of the dancing measure,
for if in the pressing stress of time

the dancer stays, or act is mime,
hands must break by being caught
as the clock covers its face with an evil weather.

Earth Descending

"This is the end," she said
and flapped from the room,
"This is the plan," she said
and twirled from the moon's
spooning and kissing and,
swishing, she fled the armourial night
and quietly said,
"I am free from the sun's orbit
and morbid regulated glances daily,
and free also from the moon's nightly
slightly sickening romances
and erased is oracular Mars and satyred Saturn
along with Pluto and the rest
of the nocturnal floral pattern.

"Now I am nothing but a spat star
and I like this high-tailing it to hell
and almost swell it is to kick up
blue dust atmospheric
(especially when one is used to
regulated black or white dust cleric).
For me right now
(and this is the end, right now)
I am pleased with these planispheric reelings
and if I were more the pig and less the planet
well, yes, dammit,
I'd squeal that this cannot, cannot
be as good as it seems
to be freed from old Electra
(and even Oedipus)
who have always hovered
and in all and every emergency
lowered the lid over the eye and me
covered with night,
(polite name for lack of sight
and of what Milton most complained)
wound me up and set me saying,
          'the end is not yet'
          'the end is not yet'

O, if they could only know
that at this moment as I splutter
and now and then twirl and flutter
into a space downward
        'upon my word!'
Quadrupled, and then again
would it be said.
O, how I would love
to bet the dear old couple
the salacious solar system
against seven buckets of the Milky Way
that this earthly eye
(it is I)
rowing wildly away
from some universal dock
with a leap in my heart which amounts
to a tick-tock clocked bomb inside me
houred for that existential arm
of the witch below
whose ripe, black brew,
smouldering and mouldering
with happy, spatted stars
is eager to receive another.

"For I, like others,
have slipped over the solar edge
spat and said,
'This is the end,
to hell with that eternal circulation
of night, day, life, death and love all over,
this is the end of an earth well worn
and born to die
and so say I
this is the end.
No need to belabour the point, however,
This is the end—and right now, moreover.'"

Lear on the Beach at Break of Day

Down on the beach at break of day
observe Lear calmly observing the sea:
he tosses the buttons of his sanity
like aged pebbles into the bay;

cold, as his sexless daughters were,
the pebbles are round by a joyless war,
worn down on a troubled, courtly ground,
they drop in the sea without a sound;

and the sea repeats their logical sin,
shedding ring after ring of watery thin
wheels of misfortune of crises shorn
which spin to no end—and never turn.

And there Lear stands, alone.
The sun is rising and the cliffs aspire.
And there Lear stands, with dark small stones
in his crazed old hands. But farther and higher

he hurls them now, as if to free
himself with them. But only stones drop
sullenly, a hardened crop,
into the soft, irrational sea.

Pain

Whether pain is simple as razors edging the fleshy cage,
Or whether pain raves with sharks inside the ribs,
It throws a bridge of value to belief
Where, towards or away from, moves intense traffic.

Or, should the eyes focus to cubes and lights of pain
And the breasts' exquisite asterisks breed circular grief,
This bird of death is radiant and complex,
Speeds fractional life over value to belief;

The bridge spans by contemporary pain
Centuries of historical birth.

And In Our Time

A world flew in my mouth with our first kiss
and its wings were dipped in all the flavours of grief.
Oh my darling, tell me, what can love mean in such a world,
and what can we or any lovers hold in this immensity
of hate and broken things?
Now it is down, down, that's where your kiss travels me,
and, as a world tumbling shocks the theories of spheres,
so this love is like falling glass shaking with stars
the air which tomorrow, or even today, will be
a slow, terrible movement of scars.

Patience

Patience is the wideness of the night
the simple pain of stars
the muffled explosion of velvet
it moves itself generally
through particulars
accepts the telling of time
without day's relativity.

But more than these accommodations
patience is love withdrawn
into the well; immersion into
a deep place where green begins.
It is the slow beat of slanting eyes
down the heart's years,
it is the silencer
and the loving now
involves no word.
Patience is the answer
poised in grief—the knowing—
it is the prose of tears
withheld and the aging,
the history in the heart
and futures where pain
is a lucid cargo.

from EVEN YOUR RIGHT EYE

Two Versions:

1. Poetry

Fidelity
      as in love
            is in poetry
                  an unexpected satisfaction.
Or, rendered into French,
                  "The Importance of Being Earnest" becomes
"L'important, c'est d'être fidèle"!
Discoverable after promiscuities,
              flirtations,
                  flights of fancy;
This is to say that
              Genius is no scarecrow!
    For instance:
              Murder in South Kensington
is not strange fruit on any poet's tree;
    For instance:
              The hoodwinked eye of ignorance
lurks sinister beneath the professorial gown;
    Or,
          Extremes of possibility are not always
the greatest possible extremities,
              for,
              like a monk in meditation
Poetry
      is cloaked in sheer
             profundities of otherness,
its ambiguous nakedness its serene capacity
            for wisdom: nothing denied
until entirely known.

           And so, in the chaste embrace
of faithful lovers
           Poetry may

              freely ravage the pulse of evil
        that throbs in the dark incestuous part
of every earnest lover's earthly heart.

2. In Situ

The poet in his tree of hell
will see life steadily and see it well.

The world is round. It moves in circles.

The poet in his vision tree
imparts immaculate necessity
to murder, ignorance and lust.

The world is round. It moves in circles.

Poetry, the poet's curse,
will look, for better or for worse,
like a simple monk in meditation

cloaked in apparent deprivation:
in its ambiguous nakedness
glows the raiment of its otherness.

The world is round. It moves in circles.

With laughter on his haunted face,
a madman captive in a leaf's embrace,
the poet wildly shakes his tree . . .

The world is round. It moves in circles.

Marvell's Garden

Marvell's garden, that place of solitude,
is not where I'd choose to live
yet is the fixed sundial
that turns me round
unwillingly
in a hot glade
as closer, closer I come to contradiction,
to the shade green within the green shade.

The garden where Marvell scorned love's solicitude—
that dream—and played instead an arcane solitaire,
shuffling his thoughts like shadowy chance
across the shrubs of ecstasy,
and cast the myths away to flowering hours
as yes, his mind, that sea, caught at green
thoughts shadowing a green infinity.

And yet Marvell's garden was not Plato's
garden—and yet—he *did* care more for the form
of things than for the thing itself—
ideas and visions,
resemblances and echoes,
things seeming and being
not quite what they were.

That was his garden, a kind of attitude
struck out of an earth too carefully attended,
wanting to be left alone.
And I don't blame him for that.
God knows, too many fences fence us out
and his garden closed in on Paradise.

On Paradise! When I think of his hymning
Puritans in the Bermudas, the bright oranges
lighting up that night! When I recall
his rustling tinsel hopes
beneath the cold decree of steel,
Oh, I have wept for some new convulsion
to tear together this world and his.

But then I saw his luminous plumèd Wings
prepared for flight,
and then I heard him singing glory
in a green tree,
and then I caught the vest he'd laid aside
all blest with fire.

And I have gone walking slowly in
his garden of necessity
leaving brothers, lovers, Christ
outside my walls
where they have wept without
and I within.

Mourning Ballad

He came to me in mourning clothes
On the day after Christmas,
Oh he came to me in the morning
To bring me his gift of kisses.

So he took off his funeral greatcoat
And removed his funereal tie,
And we laughed at his gentleman's silksocks
As he tossed them up so high

They fell on top of his darksuit
Left on the corner chair,
And we loved in the crossed hours of mourning
To make our funeral fair.

Marian Scott

If she is a moth
then all light is lured toward her,
this she consumes and becomes
the moth burning in its own light.
Brighter than all the stars and planets
her central flame transmutes
the nerveless sun into a spine of white
which darts the imageless world back into space.
Pigments she takes and breaks them into one
pearl smoking whiteness, and then eye
directs hand to flourish the first morning
into fire. The walls float from her house
and wing with paintings into all ourselves
for I have seen around her head flying
the whole career of colour,
and in her hands the age of darkness dying.
Light, oh it swims from the tragic sun
into her instant miracle
where, caught in the wire net of form,
she twists and turns it into day's
urchins and angels—
blood of our blood, bone of her luminous bone.

Old Woman

Her skin has dried and wrinkled
like a continent,
like a continent
without motion and only one season
where everything is repeated that has been said.

Her heart has dried and shrivelled
into a small ruin,
into a small ruin
her life crumbles, and only one cause—
people dying everywhere, repeating her dread.

Her hands have dried and withered
into white claws,
into white claws
with nothing to clutch, only her fear
that sleeps at her throat like her ghostly beloved.

Her eyes have failed as life failed
like dying stars,
like dying stars
her night darkens and only refers
her dyingness to darkness and a hard god.

The Mind Reader

I thought,
and he acted
upon my thought,
read by some wonderful
kind of glass my mind
saw passing that way
gulls floating over boats
floating in the bay,
and by some wonderful
sleight of hand
he ordered the gulls to land
on boats
and the boats to land.

Or, was it through waves
he sent the boats
to fly with gulls
so that out of care
they all could play
in a wonderful
gull-boat-water way
up in a land of air?

Fragment

That violet
     either in the grove
          or in the light
is the minute particle
          of an area's given growth;
Speak to that violet
          or call to the light
and what is given back
          is not echo
but the mute substance
          of the work of love.

Lament

Knowing that everything is wrong,
how can we go on giving birth
either to poems or the troublesome lie,
to children, most of all, who sense
the stress in our distracted wonder
the instant of their entry with their cry?

For every building in this world
receives our benediction of disease.
Knowing that everything is wrong
means only that we all know where we're going.

But I, how can I, I,
craving the resolution of my earth
take up my little gang of sweet pretence
and saunter day-dreary down the alleys, or pursue
the half-disastrous night? Where is that virtue
I would claim with tense impersonal unworth,
where does it dwell, that virtuous land
where one can die without a second birth?

It is not here, neither in the petulance
of my cries, nor in the tracers of my active fear,
not in my suicide of love, my dear.
That place of perfect animals and men
is simply the circle we would charm our children in
and why we frame our lonely poems in
the shape of a frugal sadness.

Double Entendre

The seed white
      beneath the flesh
           red and diamonded
               under the skin
                    rough, round,

of the round pomegranate
           hopes in essential shape
               for a constellation of fruit

Just as the pregnant woman
      in the street
           carrying her three-year-old son

is one and entire
      the tribe of woman
           weighted down by the race of man—
              always to be renewed,

For the man killed
      by the Temple clock when it fell
           told me time had not stopped—
             Oh, only for him,

              though I saw

in this unflattering
      accidental
         irony
           that he had indeed come

to a timely end
      within the courtyards of the English
           Courts of Law.

And by these exaggerations of the
      nature of the Thing

(Octavian dressed up as a boy
      dressed up as a girl
         in *Der Rosenkavalier,*

the portrait of the artist
                    holding a mirror,
or Gide
          in his *Journals*
                    writing of Stendhal's)
we come to a heightened fancy
                    and a tightened fact:
the fact that man must
                    make, make
                              bone, flesh,
a structure for his loss
                    and, like gold, take
                              seeds of meaning
                                   pitiful
                    from the dross,
For in his strange
                    peripheral orbit
                              of reality and dream
he wanders, wonders,
                    through the play within the play
                              knowing not
                                   which is the right
                                        the light
the star in the cold, staring sky,
          or the star reflected in a human eye.

from THE SEA IS ALSO A GARDEN

Mad Gardener to the Sea

Mad gardener to the sea, the moon
    rages across the sky to tend
        oceans of an unloving dark
           and the bone-blooming skeleton:
beyond all Paradise, all Arden
    moon multiplies the garden;
        nor doth the coral orchard care
           man dreameth ever back to water—
l'homme inconnu et solitaire.

Propositions

I could divide a leaf
and give you half.

Or I could search for two leaves
sending you one.

Or I could walk to the river
and look across

and seeing you there,
or not there,

absence or presence,
would spring the balance to my day.

Or I could directly find you and take your hand
so that one hand would be given

and one kept, like a split leaf
or like two leaves separate.

These would be signs and offerings:
the just passion, just encountering.

Or we perhaps could speed four eyes,
the chariot horses of our dreams and visions,

in them direction and decision find.
The split leaf floating on the river,

the hand sketching in the air
a half-moon, its hidden wholeness there.

Countered

An easy climate with all the elements,
earth, air, fire, water.
A desperate system solid as it is human.
Dust is falling where dust has climbed.
The sun is patient, moon calm,
the sin of knowledge almost innocence.
Love has become goodwill, as grief has,
as torturing strength has warped to sanity.
Now dustbowl earth completes its nothingness,
every bright image, lark or cardinal,
has dropped its wings, has moulted in disgust.
The lucid mind fumbles to doors and falls.
The crusted eyes tears cannot clarify.
But traveller dust which notices our earth
we totally invite until we die.
Now earth must spin as little as it is
as it has spun before our vast illusion.
Now loves will tumble on dark beds of space.
Loves will tumble now in any case.
But eyes of power, the long mileage to stars
our sleep will dreaden and intensify.
Lovers will love, and all the instant world
will tether joy, creation's sweet pathetic trust,
while our participating marrow
clicks with destroying dust.

Breaking

Give us wholeness, for we are broken.
But who are we asking, and why do we ask?
Destructive element heaves close to home,
our years of work broken against a breakwater.

Shattered gods, self-iconoclasts,
it is with Lazarus unattended we belong
(the fall of the sparrow is unbroken song).
The crucifix has clattered to the ground,
the living Christ has spent a year in Paris,
travelled on the Métro, fallen in the Seine.
We would not raise our silly gods again.
Stigmata sting, they suddenly appear
on every blessed person everywhere.
If there is agitation there is cause.

Ophelia, Hamlet, Othello, Lear,
Kit Smart, William Blake, John Clare,
Van Gogh, Henry IV of Pirandello,
Gerard de Nerval, Antonin Artaud
bear a crown of darkness.
It is better so.

Responsible now each to his own attack,
we are bequeathed their ethos and our death.
Greek marble white and whiter grows
breaking into history of a west.
If we could stand so virtuously white
crumbling in the terrible Grecian light.

There is a justice in destruction.
It isn't "isn't fair".
A madhouse is designed for the insane,
a hospital for wounds that will re-open,
a war is architecture for aggression,
and Christ's stigmata body-minted token.
What are we whole or beautiful or good for but to be absolutely broken?

The Time of Man

extrapolations from an article
by Dr. Loren Eiseley

"The little toe is attractive

            to the student of rudimentary
and vanishing organs,"

and whooping cranes claxon

             to the spellbound preservers
of what would naturally vanish.

When the adored ones

            pass through the door ("the future
of no invention can be guaranteed")

who does not follow them,

           half in love with his tears,
tickled by the lower brain,
         "the fossil remnant,"
               claws

    scratching at the large
           symbolic order,
animal sad, watching the members
           fade:

    clitoral love, the royal we
           stumbling:
"The perfectly adjusted perish with their environment"

    —then take me with you
          crying
            take me with you—

The brain when it began to grow

         was "shielded by a shell of bone
as thick as a warrior's helmet."

Two Pears: A Still Life

Two pears
    a slight distance over there
        unmoving within the golden
time-globe
    not by wind swung
        nor from branch suspended
but plucked
    now placed before the eyes'
        encountering where sudden love
returns
    all prodigal from arid outlands
        scrub, cactus, anguish of being.

The pears
    fruit, the first idea, seed
        into core into pulp and glowing
skin, love's
    radical contour shines here in stillness
        secret, original, a dream of candor.

Images in Crystal

Crystal cuts sharp again into the mind
as love came clear that once-upon-a-time,
so crystal takes this morning and this air,
dazzles the shadow, the sentiment, and finds
diamond calligraphy, crystalized despairs.

Venetian workers blowing that glass horse
which catches now the Paris atmosphere,
that chandelier upholding one friend's doom
reflected in the mirrors of his room;
and then the crystal slipping through the night
as Coleridge noted moonlight stops a tear;
only this burning crystal at the heart
cuts into time and daggers into near
slaying flesh, here crystal cannot come
and live endeared. Here crystal mortifies the flesh
as love withdraws inside its crystal tomb.

A thousand chandeliers flare up, a glass horse
trots through light and splinters into ruin.

The Glass Castle

The glass castle is my image for the mind
that if outmoded has its public beauty.
It can contain both talisman and leaf,
and private action, homely disbelief.
And I have lived there as you must
and scratched with diamond and gathered diamond dust,
have signed the castle's tense and fragile glass
and heard the antique whores and stoned Cassandras
call me, and I answered in the one voice I knew,
"I am here. I do not know. . . ."
but moved the symbols and polished up the view.
For who can refrain from action—
there is always a princely kiss for the Sleeping Beauty—
when even to put out the light takes a steady hand,
for the reward of darkness in a glass castle
is starry and full of glory.

I do not mean I shall not crack the pane.
I merely make a statement, judicious and polite,
that in this poise of crystal space
I balance and I claim the five gods of reality
to bless and keep me sane.

Love Story

It was easy to see what he was up to,
the grey, bundled ape,
as he sidled half-playfully
up to the baby
and with a sly look behind
put his hands onto the crib
and leapt in.

The child's pink, beginning face
stared up as the hair-handed monkey
explored the flesh, so soft, of our infant race.
The belly spread like plush to the monkey's haunch,
he settled, heavy and gay, his nuzzling
mouth at the baby's neck.

But, no answer accurate to a smile,
he bit, tasted time, maddened,
and his nails rooted sudden fire in the ribs of Adam,
towered, carnivorous, for aim
and baby face, ears, arm
were torn and taken in his ravaging.

And so the killing, too-late parents came,
hysteric, after their child's
futile pulse had stopped its beating.
Only the half-pathetic, half-triumphant
monkey peered out from the crib,
bobbed nervously on the dead infant's belly,
then stopped, suddenly paralyzed on that soft tomb.

Was it the donkey Death brayed out at him
from the human mother's eyes,
or did his love for her in that pause
consume him?

The jealous ape's death was swift
and of natural cause. "Died of shame,"
some said, others, "of shock."
But his death was Othello's death,
as great, as picayune,
he died of envy, lacking the knack of wisdom.

Sitting

The degree of nothingness
is important:
to sit emptily
in the sun
receiving fire
that is the way
to mend
an extraordinary world,
sitting perfectly
still
and only
remotely human.

A Tall Tale

The whale, improbable as lust,
carved out a cave
for the seagirl's rest;
with rest the seagirl, sweet as dust, devised
a manner for the whale
to lie between her thighs.
Like this they lay
within the shadowed cave
under the waters, under the waters wise,
and nested there, and nested there and stayed,
this coldest whale aslant the seagirl's thighs.

Two hundred years perhaps swam by them there
before the cunning waters so distilled the pair
they turned to brutal artifacts of stone
polished, O petrified prisoners of their lair.
And thus, with quiet, submerged in deathly calm,
the two disclosed a future geologic long,
lying cold, whale to thigh revealed
the secret of their comfort
to the marine weeds,
to fish, to shell, sand, sediment and wave,
to the broken, dying sun
which probed their ocean grave.
These, whale and seagirl, stone gods,
stone lust, stone grief,
interred on the sedimented sand
amongst the orange starfish,
these cold and stony mariners
invoked the moral snail
and in sepulchral voice intoned a moral tale:

"Under the waters, under the waters wise,
all loving flesh will quickly meet demise,
the cave, the shadow cave is nowhere wholly safe
and even the oddest couple can scarcely find relief:
appear then to submit to this tide and timing sea,
but secrete a skillful shell and stone and perfect be."

To Friends Who Have Also Considered Suicide

It's still a good idea.
Its exercise is discipline:
to remember to cross the street without looking,
to remember not to jump when the cars side-swipe,
to remember not to bother to have clothes cleaned,
to remember not to eat or want to eat,
to consider the numerous methods of killing oneself,
that is surely the finest exercise of the imagination:
death by drowning, sleeping pills, slashed wrists,
kitchen fumes, bullets through the brain or through
the stomach, hanging by the neck in attic or basement,
a clean frozen death—the ways are endless.
And consider the drama! It's better than a whole season
at Stratford when you think of the emotion of your
family on hearing the news and when you imagine
how embarrassed some will be when the body is found.
One could furnish a whole chorus in a Greek play
with expletives and feel sneaky and omniscient
at the same time. But there's no shame
in this concept of suicide.
It has concerned our best philosophers
and inspired some of the most popular
of our politicians and financiers.
Some people swim lakes, others climb flagpoles,
some join monasteries, but we, my friends,
who have considered suicide take our daily walk
with death and are not lonely.
In the end it brings more honesty and care
than all the democratic parliaments of tricks.
It is the "sickness unto death"; it is death;
it is not death; it is the sand from the beaches
of a hundred civilizations, the sand in the teeth
of death and barnacles our singing tongue:
and this is "life" and we owe at least this much
contemplation to our western fact: to Rise,
Decline, Fall, to futility and larks,
to the bright crustaceans of the oversky.

Eichmann Trial

Legal beauty,
frail royalty
of mind
ritualize
the paucity of means,
the ethic not undone
by legal fiction
but nearly,
the moral structure
quaking in its boots—
self-recrimination,
oaths,
fainting,
rehearsal of sorrow
contained by the gestures
of law and the error
of structural analysis.
Simultaneity, that's the
vraie politesse:
outside the court,
blaspheming pity,
horror, tears,
storm the logicians
of dispersal,
psychotic, illegal,
the embarrassing bastard
urchins of our evil.

A Long Line of Baby Caterpillars

A long line of baby caterpillars
follow their leader from the house corner
heading dead on for the Japanese Plum Tree.

Take away my wisdom and my categories!

Picasso Exhibition

Paris, 1954

In the simplicity of age
Picasso
comes finally to
the classical moon-
shaped faces of children
or, orbed in entire rainbows,
elliptical girls;
as for the anguished land-escaped
night, a spaghetti-haired hag
has eyes to burn out the stars—

and it is all as fierce
and angelic as the child-
hood of little Paloma and Claude.
Even before we look
we have bestowed our burdens,
preconceptions, the sense
of space and time—
even so,
in innocence they tour on vertical wheels
our darkest galleries of love;
we pause, smile, move along
to the past time of pink nudes
and blue-timed dawn.

Poems of Dublin

1.

The sharp street-cry
    and the floating swan
the breezing rain
        deft and swift
an old man spitting blood
    I could be attracted
and compelled by this,
    Dublin city's yeasty
and outmoded brood.

2.

Yeats sent me to Parnell
and Parnell
to the murdered
in the park,

so if Yeats is living thought
and Parnell stone,
the butchered patriots
not yet undone,

there's no denying an immediate
attempt upon our liberty,
and I'm a bastard rebel full of fret,
a wild fool in Dublin on a spree

taking treacherous photographs
of innocent statues
inventing violent images to laugh
and swagger and hullabaloo

all the crazy way down
O'Connell Street and Parnell Square—
a grimace and a frown,
a belch in the Irish air.

3.

The purple sash and tassel
of the rhetorical heart
loudly applies itself to
the soft seduction,
the Irish mind, uneasy,
moves from where it was
to where it would be,
laughing and mocking:
the large gesture,
the flung cape,
the stage draughty
but the act good.
I'd go to Dublin any day
to hear the lilt and tilt
of a broken-down playwright
in a bookstore
and, not taking anything seriously,
not even the weather,
I'd join the ranks of "The Last Romantics."

4.

Old Yeats, your cold, bitter
lyrical, marble lines
drive me into innocence, the better
rage—the rest I can divine

with my "divining heart." I feel
in the cold wash of the rain
your cool and consonantal seal
upon the honeyed hive of brain—

upon everything! The Old Abbey,
swans, the priests' secret;
in St. Stephen's Green I see
ducks dock with amphibian unregret

at the pond's edge,
their heads turned back
into immediate, sensate, sinking necks
of purple and green fluffed and rebellious plumage.

Poetics Against the Angel of Death

I am sorry to speak of death again
(some say I'll have a long life)
but last night Wordsworth's "Prelude"
suddenly made sense—I mean the measure,
the elevated tone, the attitude
of private Man speaking to public men.
Last night I thought I would not wake again
but now with this June morning I run ragged to elude
The Great Iambic Pentameter
who is the Hound of Heaven in our stress
because I want to die
writing Haiku
or, better,
long lines, clean and syllabic as knotted bamboo. Yes!

Naked Poems

star fish
fish star

Suite 1

MOVING
to establish distance
between our houses.

It seems
I welcome you in.

Your mouth blesses me
all over.

There is room.

AND
here
and here and
here
and over   and
over   your mouth

TONIGHT
quietness.   In me
and the room.

I am enclosed
by a thought

and some walls.

THE BRUISE

Again you have left
your mark.

Or we
have.

Skin shuddered
secretly.

FLIES

tonight
in this room

two flies
on the ceiling
are making
love
quietly.   Or

so it seems
down here

YOUR BLOUSE

I people
this room
with things, a
chair,   a lamp,   a
fly,   two books by
Marianne Moore.

I have thrown my
blouse on the floor.

Was it only
last night?

YOU
took

with so much
gentleness

my dark

Suite II

While you were away

I held you like this
in my mind.

It is a good mind
that can embody
perfection   with exactitude.

The sun comes through
plum curtains.

I said
the sun is gold

in your eyes.

It isn't the sun
you said.

On the floor your blouse.
The plum light
falls more golden

going down.

Tonight
quietness
in the room.

We knew

Then you must go.
I sat cross-legged
on the bed.
There is no room
for self-pity
I said

I lied

In the gold darkening
light

you dressed.

I hid my face
in my hair.

The room that held you

is still here.

You brought me clarity.

Gift after gift
I wear.

Poems   naked
in the sunlight
on the floor.

Non Linear

An instant of white roses.
                Inbreathing.
A black butterfly's
                twitch and determined
collapse on a yellow round.

near the white Tanabe
narcissus
near Layton's *Love*
daffodils
outside   falling on
the pavement
the plum blossoms
of Cypress Street

the yellow chrysanthemums

        (I hide my head when I sleep)

a stillness
in jade

        (Your hand reaches out)

the chrysanthemums

are

        (Job's moaning, is it, the dark?)

a whirlwind!

Eros! *Agapé Agapé*

Her sickness does not ebb
anyhow, it's not a sea
it's a lake largely
      moon-ridden.

I can see her perfectly clearly
through this dusk her face
the colour of moonlight.

Maybe my body, maybe I?
But when has my love
      ever been

offered exactly
and why should she be an
exception?

walking in dark

waking in dark the presence of all

the absences we have known.   Oceans.

so we are distinguished to ourselves

don't want that distinction.

I am afraid.   I said that.   I said that

for you.

My white skin
is not the moonlight.
If it is
tell me, who reads
by that light?

a curve / broken
of green
moss weed
kelp shells pebbles
lost orange rind
orange crab   pale
delicates at peace
on this sand
tracery of last night's
tide

I am listening for
the turn of the tide
I imagine it will sound
an appalled sigh
the sigh of Sisyphus
who was not happy

Hieratic sounds emerge
from the Priestess of
Motion
a new alphabet
gasps for air.

We disappear in the musk of her coming.

I hear the waves
hounding the window:
lord, they are the root waves
of the poem's meter
the waves of the
root poem's sex.
The waves of Event
(the major planets, the minor
planets, the Act)
break down at my window:
I also hear those waves.

the dead dog now
the one I saw last night
carried on a man's shoulders
down to the beach
he held it by its
dead crossed legs

I have given up
complaining

but nobody
notices

"That ye resist not
evil" falling
limp into the arms
of the oppressor
he is not undone
by the burden
of your righteousness
he has touched you

Suite of Lies

I know the way
of the pear tree
and apple tree the way
the light shines
through pear petal
apple   a light
falling into our
consanguinity

brother and sister
conjunctive and
peaceable

I use the word groves
light falling
found in the orchard
finding what fell by a
breath

brother and sister
those children

the way of what fell
the lies
like the petals
falling   drop
delicately

Some Final Questions

What are you sad about?

that all my desire goes
out to the impossibly
beautiful

Why are you standing there staring?

I am watching a shadow
shadowing a shadow

Now you are sitting doubled up in pain.
What's that for?

doubled up I feel
small like these poems
the area of attack
is diminished

What do you really want?

want the apple on the bough in
the hand in the mouth seed
planted in the brain want
to think "apple"

*I don't get it. Are you talking about
process and individuation. Or absolutes
whole numbers that sort of thing?*

Yeah

But why don't you do something?

I am trying to write a poem

Why?

Listen. If I have known beauty
let's say I came to it
asking

Oh?

from SELECTED POEMS 1954-1965

Alex

at five o'clock today Alex four years old said

I will draw a picture of you!

at first he gave me no ears and I said

you should give me ears

I would like big ears one on each side

and he added them and three buttons down the front

now I'll make your skirt wide he said and he did

and he put pins in all up and down my ribs and I waited

and he said now I'll put a knife in you

it was in my side and I said does it hurt

and No! he said and we laughed and he said

now I'll put a fire on you and he put male

fire on me in the right place then scribbled me

all into flames shouting FIRE FIRE FIRE

FIRE FIRE FIRE and I said

shall we call the fire engines and he said Yes!

this is where they are and the ladders are bending

and we made siren noises as he drew the engines on

over the page then he said the Hose! and he put

the fire out and that's better I said

and he rolled over laughing like crazy

because it was all on paper

from WILSON'S BOWL

PREFACE

Poems of Failure

I.

A picture of sweet old Prince
Kropotkin on the wall

will the little lady fall from
her chair?

'Our Meeting' out of Goodman
out of *The Empire City*

knowledge? that we are
inconsolable

and now take off from there
to leave the Flying Dutchman
coming home

let the Prince hang
the little lady float

is there a shadow following the
hand that writes
always? or for the left-handed
only?

I cannot write with my right.

I grasp what I can. The rest
is a great shadow.

Nevertheless, when the boat
moves through the islands
pushes clumsily into the dock
another chapter is written
shadow moves up the gang
plank with us is Chapter
7, 11, 13?

To be reconciled with the past
is redemption but unreal as hell
if you can't recall the beginning
and of time, who can get back there?

redemptive anthropologists, archae-
ologists, bones, stones, rings of
trees. . .

The old Prince hangs on the
wall, rain-stained edges
of the portrait

and there—up goes the little lady
and—no shadow falls

'Loyal to the silence of our impasse. . .
we look at each other. . . we do not go. . .
in the faith that we are inconsolable. . .
we are resting in this hell.'

II.

Incredible fire, irresistible grace
k, k, k, kaw, kaw.
The burning on the hillside, ineffable
smoke, 'what does not change is
the will to change'
k, k, k, kaw
the drummers' drums echoing across
the bay, they won't go away
drums or echoes.
Insurrectionary wilderness of the I
am, I will be, forcing the vision
to something other, something out
side the sleep of dreams riddled
with remembrances.
k, k, k, the Prince in his dungeon
exploring his way
why is he so saintly, the reaches
of his mind so vast and intimate?
('The main structural lines of Asia are not
north and south, or west and east; they are
from the southwest to the northeast. . . .')
Kropotkin, old Prince Peter
with your forty barges on the Amur
with your hammer in Finland
dressed up in your merchant's costume
dressed up as a *page de chambre*
dressed up as an eight-year-old Persian
Prince with real jewels in your belt for
Madame Nazimova 'who was a very beautiful
woman.' Peter, sweet Prince for Nicholas
for Alexander ('and have signed myself ever
since P. Kropotkin.')
And your Alexander, your brother, suicided
in Siberia.
Peasants in the field
the Jura watchmakers scooping out lids
you writing, speaking, hoeing your garden
greeting your friends, your mind sent out
to the people, a movement turning me to you

40 years after Sacco and Vanzetti
50th anniversary of the Russian
Revolution
your gentle words wounding me on this island,
'even now, as I was
looking on the lakes and the hillocks of Finland, new and beautiful
generalizations arose before my eyes. . . . But what
right had I to these highest joys?'

III.

Guarding me is not enough. Nor my own guardianship.
Take it all away, I can walk.
What is locked in nevertheless pounds
at the gates (he dropped his dressing-gown,
one-two and ran through the gates, the
violinist in the little grey house speeding
him with a mazurka). Do we need a guide?
Garrulous voices offend, deny, kick, condemn
what the other offers. Head bows in pain to the
blows. The ears turn off. I will not listen.
I shall not speak. Tap, tap. Tap, tap, tap.
Prisoners in the St. Peter and St. Paul fortress
sending their telex messages.
Raving below the Prince, a peasant
goes mad in his cell. The Prince is listening.
As above, so below.
I slow my lines.
I walk up and down the room which looks out
on islands and strait and do not protest
'what right have I to these highest joys?'
But my 'good masterpiece of work' does not come
'between all the harmonies of the mother nature,
under the radiant rays of sun when everything grows
so vividly in the human mind and in the heart,
love, life and all the vegetation beautifully. . . .'
                    Sacco, Dedham Jail
                    November 26, 1926
writing to his dear friend Mrs. Jack.

114

PORTRAITS

Socrates

Scientia
immaculata
I ignoramus
fiddling with
the lives of
the great
think Socrates
occasionally
a fool taking
logic for truth
likewise numerology
is not statistics
but helpful magic
in all such systems
to open the
eye of the soul
as Socrates said
being careful not
to blind it
however looking
on essences.
Now I suspect
claritas
hid from shadows
it alone cast
as it fell
upon objects
laying up
luminescence
through layers
of the ethereal
mindstuff
and for alternatives
hard-edged
heavens and
hells

slumbering on both
sides of the golden
mean. On the last
day gathered together
in his prison cell
they discussed these
matters they were
clever and even
gentle with one
another exemplary
students for the
old master
about to go who
stroking Phaedo's
locks laid a bet
(or an oath?)
concerning the length
of hair.
Whoever died like that
with such good manners?
Such elegance of
speech and
intricacy of thought?
The absolute
business
of the state
settled
good citizen Socrates
law-abiding to the
bitter end liberating
his soul through
sweet philosophy
his major music
chorded harmoniously
pluck   pluck
tuned and ready to
fly with its eye
wide open for
a new spectrum
securing melodious

ultra-violet and
infra-red
through the tip
of each wing.
The cup of hemlock
doesn't seem to cause
pain to the old man
under the blanket
in his cell surrounded
by friends. He remembers
a last obligation
(legs and torso numb)
pokes out his head
to tell Crito: 'I owe
a cock to Asclepius:
will you remember
to pay the debt?'
Even his last words
a question.
What a dumb play
for one who knew
all the answers
his questions
were answers.
'For is not philosophy
the study of death?'

For Fyodor

I am a beetle in the cabbage soup they serve up for geniuses
in the House of the Dead.

I am a black beetle and loll seductively at the bottom of the
warm slop.

Someday, Fyodor, by mistake you'll swallow me down and I'll become
a part of your valuable gutworks.

In the next incarnation I hope to imitate that idiot and saint,
Prince Myshkin, drop off my wings for his moronic glory.

Or, if I miss out on the Prince, Sonya or Dunya might do.

I'm not joking. I am not the result of bad sanitation in the
kitchen, as you think.

Up here in Omsk in Siberia beetles are not accidents but destinies.

I'm drowning fast, but even in this condition I realize your bad
tempered haughtiness is part of your strategy.

You are about to turn this freezing hell into an ecstatic emblem.
A ferocious shrine.

Ah, what delicious revenge. But take care! A fit is coming!
Now, now I'll leap into your foaming mouth and jump your tongue.
Now I stamp on this not quite famous tongue

shouting: Remember Fyodor, you may hate men but it's here in
Omsk you came to love mankind.

But you don't hear, do you: there you are writhing in epileptic
visions.

Hold your tongue! You can't speak yet. You are mine, Dostoevsky.

I aim to slip down your gullet and improve myself.
I can almost hear what you'll say:

> Crime and Punishment
> Suffering and Grace

and of the dying

> pass by and forgive
> us our happiness

Ezra Pound

And among the divine paranoids old Ezra
paces his cage unattached to the mode of doubt
replete with salvation he is 60 years old
under the Pisan sunfire. He sees straight
through the bars into the court of Confucius
then slumps in a corner wondering what went
wrong. His old man's hair is matted with rain
and wardust. His brain is in fever.
Nevertheless he hikes from pole to pole
to plot once more the stars of his fixed
obsession. It seems so clear. If only
they'd listened. They shine light all night
on the perplexity of his predicament.
He stares back, can't sleep, understands
nothing. Jew-hater. Poet. Intellectual.
A curious animal, a-typical, it reads and
writes, shaking and sweating, being so shut in,
the canto arising:
    'And if the corn cat be beaten
    Demeter has lain in my furrow'
the mode of doubt imprisoned for ever and ever
in the style of its own luxury.

Rilke

Rilke, I speak your name I throw it away
with your angels, your angels, your statues
and virgins, and a horse in a field held
at the hoof by wood. I cannot take so much
tenderness, tenderness, snow falling like lace
over your eyes year after year as the poems
receded, roses, the roses, sinking in snow
in the distant mountains.

Go away with your women to Russia or take them
to France, and take them or don't the poet is
in you, the spirit, they love that.
(I met one in Paris, her death leaning outward,
death in all forms. The letters you'd sent her,
she said, stolen from a taxi.)

Rilke.
Clowns and angels held your compassion.
You could sit in a room saying nothing,
nothing. Your admirers thought you were there,
a presence, a wisdom. But you had to leave
everyone once, once at least. That was your
hardness.

This page is a shadowed hall in Duino Castle.
Echoes. The echoes.
I don't know why I'm here.

Father

The light is mauve
my eye's iris blooms
into the nightmare of
riderless horse, the sleep honey
sings through the lilac
and I smell ash.
I touch the skin of the
horse, his pelt, thinking
of Father's military ride
Father's pomaded hair brushed
back, brown, and his long beautiful
hands holding the reins
just so, horse dancing.
And at the end, Father
smiling his great Rosicrucian smile
sniffing the light
flicked whip of lilac
his eyes seeing beyond me
the Rosy Cross.

Vasarely

for Ann Richardson

Vasarely arrives through the mail
disguised as a postcard from Aix-en-
Provence, Detroit, or Tallahassee, Fla.
He is hiding his secret vice in a cube
of mauve.

I am wrong. Vasarely is a red telephone box.
No. Vasarely is in a telephone box (blue).
He is dialing Tridim-C 1968—*Allo! Allo!*
He connects with Tallahassee and Saturday's
death in the afternoon opera.
'Pourquoi es-tu si triste ma chère?'
He is death in the afternoon.

Vasarely is no longer in his green telephone box.
He is in Sri Lanka standing on his head.
He sticks out his tongue and wriggles
his fingers in his ears.
He hates Wagner. He disappears.

He is, perhaps, an opening on
the invisible—*Allo . . . Allo . . .*

He dials again (in his index finger
the fingerprints of Mars):
'Tu es dégoutante, ma soeur!
You are the one I blame.' He hangs
up smiling.
I myself have brown eyes.

I shift my gaze from the abode of adoration.

Ach! He is a grey gnome in a playpen
dribbling integers crying
for the holy spectrum.
I would freeze him into a tray of ice-cubes
but he'd only look out at me
with his aqua eyes.

He's out and scuttling around the corner
passing among the archangels and their

sibling rivals—*Allo . . . Allo . . .*
dicing for multiples of eleven.

(Pourquoi es-tu si triste?)

He is withdrawn again into the
Everlasting, studying his *Book of
Changes,* his horrendous hexagrams.
He is laughing and laughing.

And only yesterday I thought I saw
him painting himself into a corner.
(ochre). He caught me looking.
He hopped up the ladder
and then he came down.
He fanned a pack of red.
It laid me low. It said:

*'Pourquoi es-tu si triste, chérie?
C'est toujours moi.
C'est moi. C'est Vasarely.'*

CRIMES

Treblinka Gas Chamber

Klostermayer ordered another count of the children.
Then their stars were snipped off and thrown into
the center of the courtyard. It looked like a field of
buttercups. — Joseph Hyams, *A Field of Buttercups*

fallingstars
        'a field of
                buttercups'

              yellow stars
                      of David
                              falling
the prisoners
            the children
                    falling

              in heaps
                    on one another
                              they go down
Thanatos
        showers
              his dirty breath
                      they must breathe
                                  him in
              they see stars
                    behind their
                          eyes
David's
        'a field of
                buttercups'

           a metaphor
                  where all that's
                        left lies down

Three Mile Island

Three?
  Mile?
    Island?

A Question of Questions

question
query
hook
    of the soul
    a question of
questions
              why / how
                oh God
              has it come to this
hook
sickle
scythe
    to cut us down this
mark?
    who—how many years
    to shape the mind to make
    its turn toward this?
    the where / when of the type
    the proper fall of lead
    in the printer's font?
    and who are you in this
school
room
torture chamber?
    whose are you?
    and what of your
trials and errors?
the judge
    in his echo chamber
    cannot know
    and nor can you
    you cannot answer

IV.

Extracted toenails.
I have nothing to say.

Burns on the breasts.
I have nothing to say.

Electric shock.
I have nothing to say.

Beatings.
I have nothing to say.

Refinements of an old skill.
Make the inner outer.

I am what I am.
All one.

Done. Take it away.

V. *for R.D.L.*

The error lies in
the state of desire
in wanting the answers
wanting the red-crested
woodpecker to pose
among red berries
of the ash tree
wanting its names
its habitations
the instinct
of its ways for
my head-travelling
wanting its colours
its red, white, its black
pressed behind my eyes
a triptych
three-fold
and over
and wanting the bird
to be still and
wanting it moving
whiteflash of underwings
dazzling all questions
out of me, amazement
and outbreathing
become a form
of my knowing.

I move and it moves
into a cedar tree.
I walk and I walk.
My deceiving angel's
in-shadow joins me
paces my steps and threatens
to take my head
between its hands.

I keep walking.
Trying to think.
Here on the island
there is time
on the Isabella
Point Road.
We pass a dead
deer on the beach.
Bloated. It stinks.
The angel insists, 'Keep
walking. It has all the time
in the world. Is sufficient.
Is alone. Keep walking.'
it says and flies off
with my head.

What's left of me
remembers a funny song
also a headless
man on rockface
painted in red
by Indian finger spirits.

The red-crested woodpecker swoops down
and sits on my trunk. Posing.
Dryocopus pileatus. 'Spectacular, black,
Crow-sized woodpecker with a red *crest,*
great size, sweeping wingbeats, flashing
white underwing.' Pileated woodpecker.
Posing. Many questions.
'The diggings, large *oval* or *oblong* holes,
indicate its presence.'

Zen Master.

Free Translations

I.

Raven did not come on Thursday.
He sent nothing.
Not a word. Not a sign.
Nothing on Thursday. Nothing on Friday. Nothing
on Saturday. Nothing on Sunday.
Then he sent eagles.

II.

Raven has blue eyes, like the waters of the
Queen Charlotte Islands on a good day.
He also carries a black magic umbrella.
This makes me want to sing. Caw caw.
Or cry.

III.

Raven is just a baby
floating in his cradle on the sea.
He bides his time sucking his wing
and dreaming of stone tits.
He is going to create something
great when he grows up:
the world first, ha ha.
And then his mother.

IV.

Raven has all the girls he needs.
He's got machismo and charisma.
He sings Cole Porter songs in the shower
and thinks he's James Cagney.
When he's dry he plays the piano
choosing a Chopin nocturne, so touching.

V.

Raven's got everything going for him.
He's riding high.
He says he's going to steal the sun.
Why not the sun?

Then we can all shine.

ARTIFACTS

The Bowl

This is not a bowl you drink from
not a loving cup.
This is meditation's place
cold rapture's.
Moon floats here
belly, mouth, open-one-eye
any orifice
comes to nothing
dark as any mask
or light, more light / is
holy *cirque.*
Serene, it says silence
in small fish
cups a sun
holds its shape
upon the sea
howls, 'Spirit entered
black as any raven.'
Smiles—
and cracks your smile.
Is clean.

In This Place

The spirits are not benign
up on Mt. Erskine chittering
at fog-flyers
up on Mt. Maxwell with cougar
who spies out the lambs of Musgrave.
Up on Mount Bruce mean spirits
scrabble radio waves
for living and dead.
They doze on Mt. Tuam.
They never sleep.
At full moon
they come down on the rocks
of the sea's shore
deliver such messages:
are not gone.
We quake. We draw curtains
against the word's blaze.

She goes out on the water
hearing.
Is taken or given
by tides.
I go as far as I can
collaborating in the fame.

Her scheme of last minutes
her strategies
are little songs
for great earth
(to which I listen carefully
in this place).

The Place Is Where You Find It

What was the path she took?
As winding as her gut
with the pain in it?
Along the beach?
To the caves in the hill?
Path of her mind turning
on symbols. Civility and
the Wild Woman's scream.
And horror. Horror.
Path to the beach
at full moon at last
joy of that mean water,
the manic ride out in the bay.

DREAMS AND THE COMMON GOOD

Composed Like Them

November 11, 1978

A pair of strange old birds
flew right into my dream,
Orville's and Wilbur's crates
waking me up with a start,
knocking my ivory gate,
calling me up to see
some old-time movie I knew
I never wanted to be.

Out of my past they came
creaking above Pat Bay,
come from a small backyard
in Kitty Hawk, USA. Or come
from farther away. Come from
the Ancient of Days. Tacky
old spiritual pair,
idle, extinct, and adored.

Am I the one with wings
fixed on with faulty glue?
Or am I the angelic form
doting, unfaithful, and true?
No matter who I am, I'm sure they're here to stay,
I swear their corruption's done,
their wings now silvery-grey;
moth-eaten skeletons,
odd awkwardness at play.

Out of the fire they came
into Comedic light,
dragonflight spheres of thought,
filigreed lace for my sight.
But living together so long,
aloft in the petalled night,
has muted their loon-like song
to which they had every right.

Is this what Auden knew,
that the pair are secretly bored,
cruising that River of Light,
scaring the illiterate horde?
Too old to mate, do they get
from Alighieri's shore
a voyeuristic view of this
small round polished floor
which makes us passionate,
or leaves us cold—and late?

A few feet above Pat Bay,
Dear lovers, you float upon
my childhood's airforce base,
my obsolescent song.
Old combatants up there,
hang-gliding Gemini,
yet sombre, home at last,
mechanically free,
steering your time machine
all for the likes of me.

I the dreamer dream
this flight at 51,
I, astonished and awed
under the moon and sun;
I, under the supernova,
asleep on the small round floor,
hear cackles of Zennish laughter
riming ecstatic puns.
I with my *Vita Nuova,*
I with my lines undone.

Metaphysics of Spring

Blossoms—
powder of pink
moths, sift
of mystic wind-
watchers
shift of desire's
bled light
gloss of—ah, gross
matter (great
matter), it does
not, even
matter
burning / the
shudder of / in
the wings!
in shell's pink
growing, birth
of the world
/ feathery
flesh or love
what matter?

Eschatology of Spring

Death, Judgement, Heaven, Hell,
and Spring. The Five Last Things,
the least of which I am, being in
the azaleas and dog-toothed violets
of the South of Canada. Do not tell me
this is a cold country. I am also in
the camelias and camas of early, of
abrupt birth.
We are shooting up for the bloody
judgement of the six o'clock news.
Quick, cut us out from the deadlines
of rotting newspapers, quick, for the
tiny skeletons and bulbs will tell you
how death grows and grows in Chile and
Chad. Quick, for the small bones pinch
me and insects divulge occult excrement
in the service of my hyacinth, my trailing
begonia. And if you catch me resting
beside the stream, sighing against
the headlines of this pastoral, take
up your gun, the flowers blossoming
from its barrel, and join this grief, this
grief: that there are lambs, elegant black-
footed lambs in this island's eschatology,
Beloved.

The Days of the Unicorns

I remember when the unicorns
roved in herds through the meadow
behind the cabin, and how they would
lately pause, tilting their jewelled
horns to the falling sun as we shared
the tensions of private property
and the need to be alone.

Or as we walked along the beach
a solitary delicate beast
might follow on his soft paws
until we turned and spoke the words
to console him.

It seemed they were always near
ready to show their eyes and stare
us down, standing in their creamy
skins, pink tongues out
for our benevolence.

As if they knew that always beyond
and beyond the ladies were weaving them
into their spider looms.

I knew where they slept
and how the grass was bent
by their own wilderness
and I pitied them.

It was only yesterday, or seems
like only yesterday when we could
touch and turn and they came
perfectly real into our fictions.
But they moved on with the courtly sun
grazing peacefully beyond the story
horns lowering and lifting and
lowering.

I know this is scarcely credible now
as we cabin ourselves in cold
and the motions of panic
and our cells destroy each other
performing music and extinction
and the great dreams pass on
to the common good.

from TALKING

Field Guide to Snow Crystals

       —stellar rime
    star crystals   in a sunfield
of snow. No
          two crystals exactly alike (like
me and the double I've never known
          or the four-leaf clover)
    a down drifting

of snow
      spatial dendrites
         irregular germs

snow grows
     scales skeletons fernlike extensions
        needles scrolls
           and
          sheaths branches

lightly or heavily
     rimed
stars on cold ground shining
        ice lattice!

For the field guides me/my
        flutterhand
   to a fistful of
      plates clusters minute columns
     Graupel-like snow of lump type
      solid and hollow bullets
       cup

cupped in my hand
      thrown across a field
  "or. . . a series of fields folded"

 a ball   star
("tiny columns and plates fallen from very cold air")

a quick curve into
                sky/my
                        surprised
    winterbreath
            a *snowflake*
        caught midway in your throat—

from SUNDAY WATER: THIRTEEN
ANTI GHAZALS

I watch the pile of cards grow.
I semaphore for help (calling stone-dead John Thompson).

A mist in the harbour. Hydrangea blooms turn pink.
A game of badminton, *shuttlecock*, hitting at feathers!

My family is the circumstance I cannot dance with.
At Banff I danced in black, so crazy, the young man insisting.

Four or five couplets trying to dance
into Persia. Who dances in Persia now?

A magic carpet, a prayer mat, red.
A knocked off head of somebody on her broken knees.

Heidegger, notes of music
in his name.

The rose blooms because it blooms in the trellis.
A scale of black death because a scale of black death.

Around me, little creakings
of the house. Day's end.

The universe opens. I close.
And open, just to surprise you.

Come loves, little sheep, into
the barricades of the Fall Fair.

144

Mrs. Olsson at 91 is slim and sprightly.
She still swims in the clamshell bay.

Around the corner, Robin hangs out big sheets
to hide her new added on kitchen from the building inspector.

I fly from the wide-open mouth of the seraphim.
Something or somebody always wants to improve me.

Come down, eagle, from your nifty height.
Let me look you in the eye, Mr. America.

Crash—in the woods at night.
Only a dead tree falling.

Ten white blooms on the sundeck.
The bees have almost all left. It's September.

The women writers, their heads bent under the light,
work late at their kitchen tables.

Winter breathes in the wings of the last hummingbird.
I have lost my passion. I am Ms. Prufrock.

So. So. So. Ah—to have a name like *Wah*
when the deep purple falls.

And you have sent me a card
with a white peacock spreading its tail.

My morning poem destroyed by the good neighbour policy.
Mrs. Olsson, organic gardener, lectures me on the good life.

Damned dark hole! Rabbit
in her rabbit warren, pushing them out.

Oh this *is* cozy, all of us together watching
the news, catching each other's tics and flickers.

The square ring on her third finger, six seed pearls.
On her right index finger, tiny diamond-shaped jade.

The grand design. The setting sun.
All the big animals turn towards the Great Wall of China.

Evening Autumn closes in. African marigolds
shine on. Harvest moons.

Land's End. I don't believe it. Down there—
among the reeds: cities of light and water.

From Russia, three embroidered velvet hats.
A balalaika. A necklace of amber beads.

The wood still has to be split, but I am off
again, into the air, flying East

with poems *From the Country of Eight Islands.* Hokku.
Haiku. Chōka. Kanshi. Kouta. Tanka. Renga. *Seeds.*

RECENT WORK

Edmonton Centre, Sept. 23/80

It was just there. It? They? Music
suddenly I come upon the
                              key cutting shop
and "Wool" and a young bassist—bronzed hair long
beyond her waist
                    Music
in the courtyard of the Centre. One can smoke
and listen to Music with little kids
lying on stomachs
                              escalator climbing with surprised
mid-day Edmontonians playing it cool
        who look askance
                              or turn around as the
Music mounts with them into leafy levels
of Marks and Spencers
                         staring—
The Edmonton Symphony in plain clothes fiddling
the bad vibes of Eatons and Woodwards, key shop
grinding out keys.
                    Keys!
And after the final number I'm sure I see
Maureen Forrester licking a vanilla ice-cream cone
—she waves her musical hand to a friend in the winds.
Man in cowboy hat wanders off. Chinese gentleman
moves urgently towards "Exit." Maureen takes
the escalator, strolls into Mappins.

Touchstone. She is touchstone. Remember Maureen
the Trout Quintet that summmer of '51 in Montreal?

But maybe it isn't Forrester, after all. Thirty
years later, almost, I am here
carrying nonbiodegradable plastic shopping bags
back
        to the scarey carpark
                              jangling my keys

Prison Report

The eye of Jacobo Timerman looks through the hole and sees
another eye looking through a hole.

These holes are cut into steel doors in prison cells in Argentina.

Both eyes are wary.
They disappear.

Timerman rests his cheek on the icy door,
amazed at the sense of space he feels—the joy.

He looks again: the other's eye is there,
then vanishes like a spider.

Comes back, goes, comes back.

This is a game of hide-and-seek.
This is intelligence with a sense of humour.
Timerman joins the game.

Sometimes two eyes meet at exactly the same moment.

This is music. This is love
playing in the middle of a dark night
in a prison in Argentina.

My name is Jacobo one eye says.
Other eye says something, but Jacobo can't quite catch it.

Now a nose appears in the vision-field
of Timerman. It rubs cold edges of the hole,
a love-rub for Jacobo.

This is a kiss, he decides, a caress,
an emanation of solitude's tenderness.

In this prison everything is powered electrically
for efficiency and pain. But tenderness is also
a light and a shock.

An eye, a nose, a cheek resting against a steel door
in the middle of the dark night.
These are parts of bodies, parts of speech,
saying,
I am with you.

I Daniel

for Timothy Findley

I.

But I Daniel was grieved
and the vision of my head troubled me,

and I do not want to keep
the matter in my heart

for the heart of the matter
is something different.

Neither do I want happiness
without vision.

I am apocryphal and received.
I live now and in time past

among all kinds of musick—sackbut,
cornet, flute, psaltery, harp, and dulcimer.

You come bearing jobs and treachery and money,

but I Daniel, servant to powers
that pass all understanding,

grieve into time, times, and the dividing of time.

II.

I also serve the kings,
but my own name fascinates me

with its slippery syllables.
I live in a mysterious book;

my imitators incline me to derision
for they too are fascinated by my name,

by the flagrant musick of the old lore,
sackbut and psaltery, by the grief

in all my actions.

III.

The coin is dropped into my palm.
I become the messenger, see —

here, now in my own hand
the printout of the King's text

which he has forgotten
and I remember.

Listen, I dream the dream,
I deliver its coded message

and pocket the coin.
Keep your jobs and dollars.

I go into the dark on the King's business
and spend my time thanking him

for the privilege of my servitude.

IV.

The musick of the dulcimer was a silver bird
flying about my ears

when I closed my eyes and sealed them.
Nebuchadnezzar

tapped me on the shoulder
after I'd done the job;

but all I could hear was bird
song in the apparatus,

all I could hear were three notes
from the string of the dulcimer

and one on the cornet.

V.

I ate no pleasant bread. The fast
unbroken for weeks,

then I Daniel looked and saw—
but what do you care for the grief

of what I Daniel understood by
books the number of the years of desolation?

Confusion of faces, yours among them,
the poetry tangled, no vision of my own to speak of.

The hand moved along the wall.
I was able to read, that's all.

VI.

I, even I Daniel, whose countenance
changed, said nothing about a broken heart.

Always it was the dangerous ones
who needed me

in the garden, under the stars—
always I found what they needed

flat on my face in a deep sleep:
"Messenger, here is your message."

And I Daniel fainted
and was sick certain days.

VII.

In those days I Daniel
was mourning three full weeks.

Haunted by numbers: what "passed seven
times," and what "shall be for a time,

and times, and a half"? Four horns or one
or one becoming four in the breakdown

of the bicameral mind—wherein I Daniel
alone saw the vision—

VIII.

It was only politics, wars and rumours
of war in the vision or dream:

four beasts of terror with their
numbers game. I play and trick my way

out of this scene into the arms of Gabriel
who does not hear the tune performed

on sackbut, psaltery, harp and dulcimer.

Notes to the Poems

From Trio

Chung Yung. "The word *Chung* signifies what is bent neither to one side nor to the other. The word *yung* signifies unchanging. What exists plumb in the middle is the just process of the universe and that which never wavers or wobbles is the calm principle in its mode of action." Ernest Fenellosa.

From Wilson's Bowl

Poems of Failure. I. *The Empire City*, a novel by Paul Goodman, was the beginning of my interest in anarchism. 'The little lady' (who could levitate) and the 'Flying Dutchman' are both characters in the novel. The quotations at the end of this section are from Part 3, Ch. 12, 'The Dead of Spring.' (*The Empire City*, The Bobbs-Merrill Co., Inc., New York, 1959).

II. Two basic works on the life of Kropotkin are *Memoirs of a Revolutionist* by Peter Kropotkin, ed. James Allen Rogers (Peter Smith, Gloucester, Mass., 1967), and *The Anarchist Prince* by George Woodcock and Ivan Avakumovic (T.V. Boardman & Co., Ltd., London, 1950). Kropotkin was, among many other things, a gifted geographer and explorer with particular interest in eastern Siberia. 'Poems of Failure,' II and III telescope some of the major events in his life.

III. The quotation at the end of the poem is from *The Letters of Sacco and Vanzetti*, ed. Marion D. Frankfurter and Gardner Jackson (E.P. Dutton & Co., Inc., New York, 1960).

A Question of Questions. V. 'If the dominant phantasy in this particular group was that the therapist had 'the answer' and that if they could get 'the answer' they would not be suffering. The therapist's task, like a Zen Master's, is to point out that their suffering is not due to their getting 'the answer' from him, but is in the state of desire they are in, whereby they posit the existence of 'an answer' and are frustrated because they do not seem to be getting it.' I am indebted to R.D. Laing (*The Self and Others*, Tavistock Publications, London, 1961, p. 114) for the inspiration for this poem—as well as the red-crested woodpecker. The description of *dryocopus pileatus* comes from Roger Tory Peterson's *Field Guide to Western Birds* (Houghton-Mifflin Co., Boston, 1961).

Wilson's Bowl. My friendship with Lilo Berliner sprang out of our mutual interest in petroglyphs—Indian rock carvings. Before she committed suicide she left her letters from the noted anthropologist, Wilson Duff, on my doorstep. Their correspondence had a peculiar intimacy, perhaps made possible by the fact that they never met. These poems are my attempt to deal with Lilo's obsessions and death.

The Place Is Where You Find It. 'Wild Woman'—Indian mythological figure, Tsonoqua, or 'wild-woman-of-the-woods.'

Composed Like Them. This poem arrived first as pure rhythm and meter, and though I disliked the movement I went with it to discover it was a rough parody of W.H. Auden's meter in 'September 1, 1939.' There are also references to Dante's *The Divine Comedy*, '*The Paradiso,*' *Canto* XXII where the earth is seen by Dante and Beatrice from the eighth heaven as:

The small round floor which makes us passionate
I, carried with the eternal Twins, discerned,
From hill to harbour, plain to contemplate:
Then to the beauteous eyes my eyes returned.
(trans. Laurence Binyon)

The Days of The Unicorns. 'paws': dream overlap of lion and unicorn.

From Sunday Water: Thirteen Anti Ghazals

These poems, composed between November 27 and November 29, 1981, were written on unlined file cards (6"x4" and 3"x5"), beginning as an exercise in the Ghazal form and ending in a quiet storm of six on Sunday, November 29.

In the previous spring I had belatedly discovered the Ghazals of John Thompson in *Stiltjack*, published posthumously by Anansi in 1978. Knowing little more about this ancient Persian form than what Thompson had said in his preface, my plan was to write one a day, though I usually wrote more than one when I stayed with the discipline. The plan was interrupted for most of October and November. But as I learnt more about Ghazals, I saw I was actually defying some of the traditional rules, constraints, and pleasures laid down so long ago.

"Drunken and amatory" with a "clandestine order," the subject of the traditional Ghazal was usually love, the Beloved representing not a particular woman but an idealized and universal image of Love. The couplets (usually a minimum of five) were totally unlike the conventional English couplet and were composed with an ear and an eye to music and song.

Mine tend toward the particular, the local, the dialectical and private. There are even a few little jokes. Hence "anti Ghazals." And yet in the end (though I hope to write more), Love returns to sit on her "throne of *accidie*," a mystical power intrudes, birds sing, a Sitar is plucked, and the Third Eye, opal, opens.

Biography

Phyllis Webb was born on April 8, 1927, in Victoria, B.C. In 1949, she graduated from the University of British Columbia with a B.A. in English and Philosophy, and during that same year she ran as a CCF candidate in the provincial elections. While studying at U.B.C., Webb had been reading widely in Canadian poetry and was part of an off-campus writing group led by Earle Birney. P.K. Page, E.J. Pratt and Birney were early Canadian influences, but the most important was to be F.R. Scott, whom she met while campaigning for the CCF. In 1950, Webb moved to Montreal, where she completed a year of graduate studies at McGill University—an experience which consolidated her commitment to writing. Between 1951 and 1956, Webb lived for the most part in Montreal, in the milieu of Louis Dudek (who introduced her to American poetry), Eli Mandel, Irving Layton, Miriam Waddington and Leonard Cohen. The poems in *Trio* (which also contained poems by Gael Turnbull and Eli Mandel) were composed in Montreal and published by Contact Press in 1954. *Even Your Right Eye*, written while Webb was travelling and living in England and Ireland, was published in 1956 by McClelland and Stewart as one of their Indian File series. During the years in Montreal, Webb supported herself with various secretarial jobs and by freelance broadcasting for the CBC. Her talent in the latter field eventually led to a full-time career with the CBC in the mid-1960's. *Talking* (Quadrant Editions, 1982) is a record of some of Webb's work as reviewer, broadcaster, and writer.

In 1957, Webb won a Canadian Government Overseas Award which permitted her to live in Paris and to explore her fascination with French drama and theatre. She returned to Canada after a year and a half in France, and by 1961, had begun teaching in the English

Department at U.B.C. In 1962, Ryerson Press published *The Sea Is Also a Garden.*

Inspired by the 1963 Poetry Conference at U.B.C., which brought together poets from Vancouver, Black Mountain, and San Francisco, and wanting to solve (in her words) "the problem of sentence structure" in her own work, Webb applied for and received a grant from the Canada Council. She envisioned two books at the end of the grant period: *Naked Poems,* and a book composed of long lines. To this end she travelled to the U.S. and lived for a time in San Francisco, where she read assiduously and kept extensive notebooks. *Naked Poems* (Periwinkle Press) appeared in 1965. In 1964, having accepted a job as Program Organizer in Public Affairs for the CBC, Webb moved to Toronto. In 1967, she became Executive Producer of the program "Ideas," the most distinguished series of programs of its kind in Canadian broadcasting history. On a six-month leave from "Ideas," Webb escaped to the West Coast and discovered Salt Spring Island as a place for writing and revitalization. Taking the long way back to Toronto, Webb stayed for a short time in Russia, having become interested in the anarchist movement, contemporaneous with the Russian revolution. It is around this movement that her larger narrative and historical concerns, and her experiments with a longer line and form, were beginning to gather.

After five years with the CBC, and four years after the publication of *Naked Poems*, Webb resigned from her job and fled to Vancouver "to save her soul" and began writing again. She again found sanctuary on Salt Spring Island, which was eventually to become her permanent home. By this time, Webb had begun work on the "Kropotkin Poems". In 1971, her *Selected Poems 1954-1965* (edited and with an introduction by John Hulcoop) was published by Talonbooks.

The decade of the 1970's was a difficult period for Webb. She withdrew, becoming at times reclusive, obsessed with the failure of the Kropotkin poems to fully materialize. There were the suicides of Wilson Duff and of her friend Lilo Berliner within two years of the stunning exhibition organized by Duff in 1975, "Images Stone B.C.: Thirty Centuries of North West Coast Indian Sculpture." Berliner had left her correspondence with Duff on Webb's doorstep the night she walked into the sea, and Webb's essay, "A Correspondence," published in *Talking*, is a decoding of this strange legacy. The essay is also an important commentary on the imagery and mythology of North West

Coast Indian art and culture. But out of the crisis of these years, the poems collected in *Wilson's Bowl* appeared, published by Coach House Press in 1980. Of the difficulty of these years, Webb writes in her Foreword to *Wilson's Bowl*:

> My poems are born out of great struggles of silence. This book has been long in coming. Wayward, natural and unnatural silences, my desire for privacy, my critical hesitations, my critical wounds, my dissatisfactions with myself and the work have all contributed to a strange gestation.

During this "strange gestation", Webb held various teaching jobs. In 1976-77, she taught Creative Writing at U.B.C.; and in 1977-78, she taught English and Creative Writing at The University of Victoria. As Visiting Assistant Professor in the Creative Writing Department at The University of Victoria, Webb taught again in 1978-79. *Wilson's Bowl* was published while Webb was writer-in-residence at The University of Alberta, and during the summer of 1981, she taught at the Banff School of Fine Arts. Webb is presently living and writing on Salt Spring Island, B.C.

Bibliography

Books

Trio (with Eli Mandel and Gael Turnbull) (Montreal, Contact Press, 1954
Even Your Right Eye (Toronto, McClelland and Stewart, 1956)
The Sea Is Also a Garden (Toronto, Ryerson Press, 1962)
Naked Poems (Vancouver, Periwinkle Press, 1965)
Selected Poems 1954-1965 (Vancouver, Talonbooks, 1971)
Wilson's Bowl (Toronto, Coach House Press, 1980)
Talking (Montreal, Quadrant Editions, 1982)
Sunday Water: Thirteen Anti Ghazals (Lantzville, Island Writing
  Series, 1982)

Acknowledgements

The author wishes to acknowledge the assistance of the Canada Council.